Contents

Any words appearing in the text in bold, **like this**, are explained in the glossary. You can also look out for them in 'Body language' at the bottom of each page.

Get on, move on!

Are you moving? You may be sitting quietly. But the inside of your body is never still. You are breathing. Your heart is beating. Muscles are working all the time. They are keeping you alive.

On the go

More muscles are at work when you turn this page or stand up. These muscles pull on your bones. Running, jumping, and many other movements are made in this way.

This cyclist is pushing, leaning, ➤ and twisting at the same time. All these movements are made by muscles pulling bones. The result is an amazing cycling stunt.

Body Talk

Move Your Body

BONES AND MUSCLES

EXPRESS EDITION

Steve Parker

Raintree

www.raintreepublishers.co.uk
Visit our website to find out more information about **Raintree** books.

To order:
☎ Phone 44 (0) 1865 888113
🖹 Send a fax to 44 (0) 1865 314091
💻 Visit the Raintree bookshop at **www.raintreepublishers.co.uk**
to browse our catalogue and order online.

First published in Great Britain by Raintree,
Halley Court, Jordan Hill, Oxford, OX2 8EJ,
part of Harcourt Education.
Raintree is a registered trademark of Harcourt
Education Ltd.

Produced for Raintree Publishers by
 Discovery Books Ltd
Editorial: Kathryn Walker, Melanie Waldron,
 Rosie Gordon, and Megan Cotugno
Design: Philippa Jenkins, Lucy Owen,
 John Walker, and Rob Norridge
Illustrations: Darren Linguard, Jeff Edwards
Picture Research: Mica Brancic and
 Ginny Stroud-Lewis
Production: Chloe Bloom
Originated by Modern Age Repro
Printed and bound in China by South China
Printing Company

10-digit ISBN: 1 406 20417 X (hardback)
13-digit ISBN: 978 1 4062 0417 9 (hardback)
10 09 08 07

10-digit ISBN: 1 406 20424 2 (paperback)
13-digit ISBN: 978 1 4062 0424 7 (paperback)
10 09 08 07

**British Library Cataloguing in
Publication Data**
Parker, Steve
 Move your body! : bones and muscles. - (Body
talk)
 1.Bones - Juvenile literature 2.Muscles -
Juvenile literature
I.Title
 612.7
A full catalogue record for this book is available
from the British Library.

This levelled text is a version of *Freestyle: Body
Talk: Move Your Body*

Acknowledgements
The publishers would like to thank the following
for permission to reproduce photographs:
Alamy Images **pp. 24-25** (Aflo Foto Agency),
pp. 4-5 (Buzz Pictures), **pp. 28-29** (UKraft);
Corbis **pp. 12-13, 14-15, 16-17, 24-25, 26-27,
32-33, 36-37, 38-39** (Anders Ryman), **pp. 26-27**
(Arko Datta/Reuters), **pp. 40-41** (Cheque),
pp. 20-21, 34-35 (Duomo), **pp. 10-11**
(Eric Gaillard/ Reuters), **pp. 36-37L** (Michael
Wong), **pp. 34-35** (Roy Morsch), **pp. 14-15**
(Tracy Kahn); Getty Images **pp. 30-31** (Allsport
Concepts), **pp. 10-11** (PhotoDisc), **32-33**
(Photographers' Choice), **pp. 10-11, 34-35**
(The Image Bank); Science Photo Library
pp. 18-19. 42-43; pp. 8-9 (Andrew Syred/
MANFRED KAGE), **pp. 14-15** (BSIP Dr T Pichard),
pp. 20-21 (Chris Bjornberg), **pp. 28-29**
(Clara Franzini Armstrong), **pp. 42-43**
(Damien Lovegrove), **pp. 18-19** (Dave Roberts),
pp. 22-23 (David Gifford), **p. 24** (Dept. of
Clinical Radiology, Salisbury District Hospital),
pp. 20-21 (Mehau Kulyk), **pp. 6-7** (Pasieka),
pp. 26-27 (Sheila Terry). Cover photograph of
man in dance pose reproduced with permission
of Getty Images/Stone/Ryan McVay.

The author and publisher would like to thank
Ann Fullick for her assistance in the preparation
of this book.

The paper used to print this book comes from
sustainable resources.

Disclaimer
All the Internet addresses (URLs) given in this
book were valid at the time of going to press.
However, due to the dynamic nature of the
Internet, some addresses may have changed, or
sites may have ceased to exist since publication.
While the author and publishers regret any
inconvenience this may cause readers, no
responsibility for any such changes can be
accepted by either the author or the publishers.

Dedicated to the memory of Lucy Owen

Working together

Without bones you would be a heap on the floor. Bones give you a framework. Muscles give you the power to move. But there is another body part you need for moving. You need your brain.

Your brain controls your muscles and actions. It learns to make new movements. It easily makes older ones. Try one now – turn the page!

Find out later ...

...why your nose is so squashy.

...how many muscles a body builder has.

...how complicated it is to throw a ball.

5

Let's get bones!

You have more than 200 bones in your body. Together they form your skeleton. A skeleton holds you up. Without it you would be floppy and helpless.

Skeleton from top to toes

At the top of the skeleton is your **skull**. The skull forms a case that protects your brain. It also gives shape to your face.

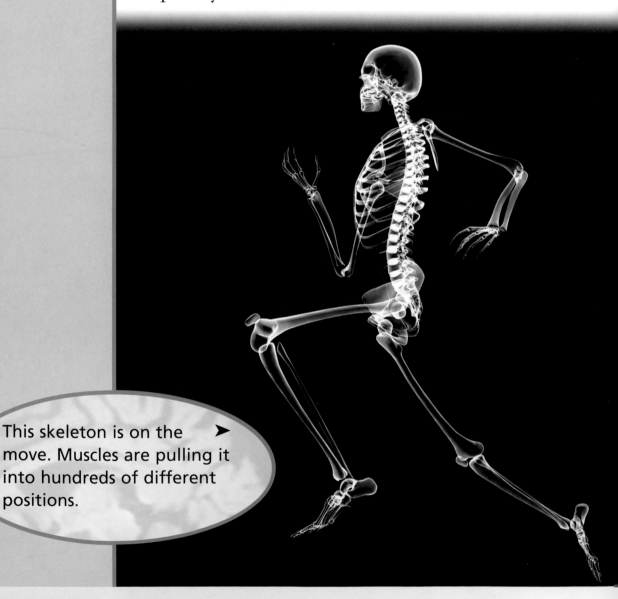

This skeleton is on the ▶ move. Muscles are pulling it into hundreds of different positions.

skull   main bone inside the head. It is really more than 20 separate bones joined firmly together.

Below your skull is your central support. This is your backbone or **spine**. Shoulder and arm bones are on each side of it. At the bottom are the hip bones. Leg bones link to these.

So many shapes

Each bone has a special shape. Arm and leg bones are long and slim. This makes them suitable for movements such as lifting and walking. Shoulder and hip bones are wide and flat. Powerful leg and arm muscles can attach to them.

When "bone" is not bone

Some parts of the skeleton are not bone. They are made of a softer, bendier substance. This is **cartilage** or "gristle". Part of each rib is made of cartilage (see below).

BONE RECORDS

- **Longest bone: the thigh bone (femur). This forms one-quarter of your total body height.**
- **Smallest bone: the stirrup bone (stapes). It is deep in the ear and is just 3 mm (1/8 inch) high.**

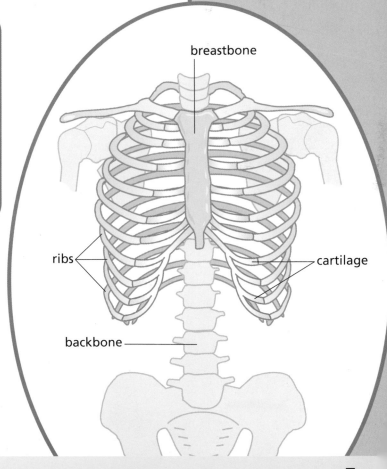

breastbone

ribs

cartilage

backbone

cartilage tough, springy substance. It covers the ends of bones inside a joint. It also forms some parts of the skeleton.

Bones alive

Old bones in a museum look dry and cracked. But bones inside a living body are tough. They are also slightly bendy. They are very much alive.

Bones have **blood vessels**. These are tubes that carry blood. They bring substances that the bone needs to stay healthy. Bones also have **nerves**. Nerves carry messages around the body. These nerves tell the brain if bones are pressed or bent.

This is the inside of a bone ➤ seen under a powerful microscope. In the centre you can see tiny blood vessels and nerves (shown in red).

blood vessels   tubes that carry blood through the body

What's in a bone?

A bone is made up of millions of tiny strings and crystals. The stringy material is called **collagen**. The crystals are made of **minerals**. Minerals are substances that the body gets from food.

A bone also contains **cells**. Cells are like tiny "building blocks". Your body is made of billions of them. Bone cells make the strings and crystals. They keep the bone healthy.

Inside a bone

Most bones have three layers. The outside is a very strong material. This is called compact bone. The middle layer is like hard sponge. In the centre is a soft, jelly-like substance. This is **bone marrow**.

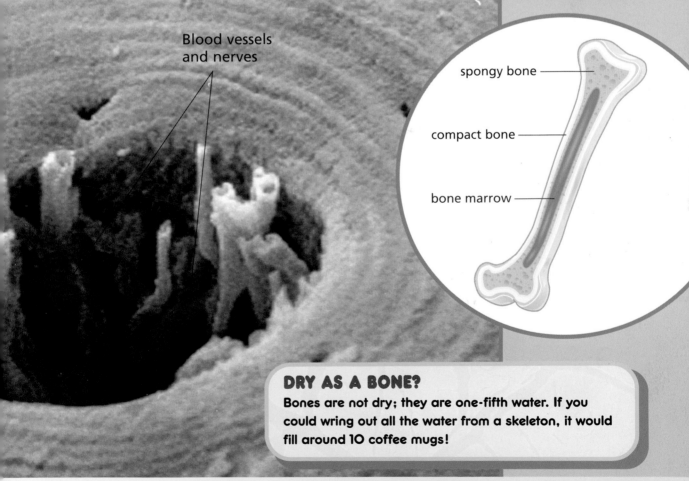

Blood vessels and nerves

spongy bone

compact bone

bone marrow

DRY AS A BONE?

Bones are not dry; they are one-fifth water. If you could wring out all the water from a skeleton, it would fill around 10 coffee mugs!

collagen   tough, string-like fibres found in body parts such as skin and bones

Bone head

The main bone inside your head is the **skull**. In fact, the skull is not one single bone. It is made up of 22 bones. Twenty-one of these are firmly fixed together. The other one bone can move.

Where's your nose?

Pictures of dead skulls usually have no noses or ears. This is because noses and ears are made of **cartilage**. This is softer and bendier than bone. It does not last as long as bone after death.

MORE BONES

These are some of the bones of the skull.

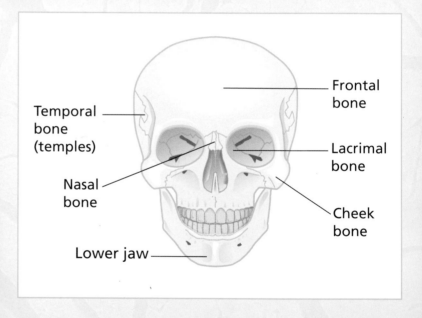

Temporal bone (temples)

Nasal bone

Frontal bone

Lacrimal bone

Cheek bone

Lower jaw

cartilage tough, springy substance. It covers the ends of bones inside a joint. It also forms some parts of the skeleton.

In your face!

The only part of your skull that can move is your lower jaw. It moves as you eat and talk.

The jaw joints are just below the ears. Eight of the other skull bones form a dome shape. This is called the **cranium**. It protects your brain. The other 13 fixed-together bones are inside your face.

▼ After death, bones are the parts that last longest. For many years the skull has been used as a sign of danger and death.

I recognise you!

Look at your family and friends. Notice how their faces differ. Skull bones are the main reason for these differences. They give your face its shape.

cranium   domed upper part of the skull

Stand up straight

One second you stand up straight. The next you can bend almost double. You can do this because you have a bendy backbone, or **spine**.

The spine is your body's central support. It is made up of 26 separate bones. These are called **vertebrae**. One sits on top of another. They are joined like links in a chain.

Cushions in the spine

The bones in your spine are separated by discs. These discs are made of **cartilage**. This is a strong, bendy material. The discs act like cushions. They also hold the bones apart.

▼ Sometimes a disc gets squeezed out of position. It presses on a **nerve** and causes pain. This is called a "slipped disc".

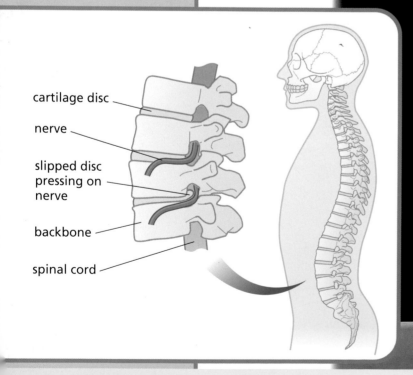

cartilage disc

nerve

slipped disc pressing on nerve

backbone

spinal cord

nerves   string-like parts that carry messages around the body

What a nerve!

The spine is hollow like a bendy tube. Your **spinal cord** runs inside it.

The spinal cord connects your brain with the rest of your body. It carries messages to your brain. These tell the brain what your skin can feel.

The spinal cord also carries messages from your brain to your muscles. These tell the muscles when to move.

◄ With proper teaching and practice, some people can bend their backs more than normal.

spinal cord   main nerve linking the brain to the rest of the body

More jobs for bones

Bones hold you up and let you move about. They do another job too. They protect your soft inside parts.

Your brain is your most precious body part. It is protected by your **skull**. The **spinal cord** (see page 13) is also well-protected. Your backbone protects it from being squeezed and knocked.

Extra help

A hard knock could break the skull. This might damage the brain. People such as cyclists, builders, and climbers risk head injury. They wear helmets or hard-hats for extra protection.

spinal cord   main nerve linking the brain to the rest of the body

Inside a cage

Your heart and lungs work together to keep you alive. They are protected by the backbone, ribs, and breastbone.

Together, these bones form a "cage" around the heart and lungs. Also, this cage can move. Your ribs move up and out as you breathe in. This allows your lungs to get bigger as they fill with air.

Small shield

The kneecap is a small bone that works as a protector. It is like a little shield. It guards the knee joint (see below).

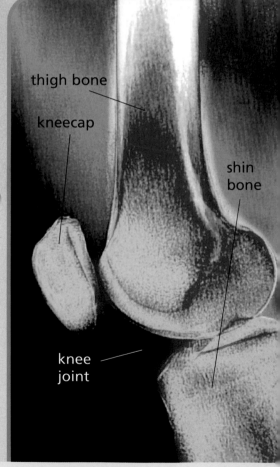

thigh bone

kneecap

shin bone

knee joint

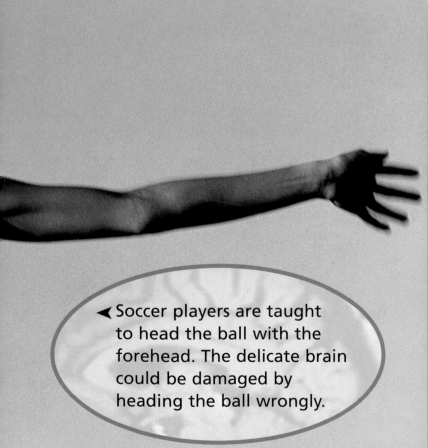

◄ Soccer players are taught to head the ball with the forehead. The delicate brain could be damaged by heading the ball wrongly.

Busy bones

Bones are very busy! They hold you up. They protect you. Many of them also make blood.

Blood contains tiny parts called **cells**. It contains **red blood cells** and **white blood cells**. Red blood cells carry **oxygen** around your body. Oxygen is a gas that our bodies need to stay alive. White blood cells fight germs and diseases.

> **BONE MINERALS**
> The body contains these minerals. They are found mainly in the bones.
> • Calcium
> • Phosphorus
> • Magnesium

Most fish contain lots of ➤ minerals. These include calcium, iodine, and magnesium. You need these for healthy bones.

oxygen   gas that makes up one-fifth of air

Millions of these blood cells die every minute. But millions more are made in your bones. They are made in a jelly-like substance. This is called **bone marrow**.

Stores

Your body needs **minerals** to stay healthy. Minerals are substances you get from food. Bones store important minerals. There may be a time when you don't get enough of them in your food. Then your body can use these stores.

Bigger bones

Calcium is a mineral. It helps make healthy, tough bones. Milk contains plenty of calcium.

minerals   substances, such as iron and calcium, that the body needs to stay healthy

Growing bones

When you were born you had about 350 bones. As an adult, you will only have 206. What is going on?

A baby's bones are made of a slightly soft, bendy substance. This is **cartilage**. As a baby grows, some cartilage bones join. They form larger bones.

Some cartilage bones slowly turn into real bone. When you are about 20 years old, your skeleton will be nearly all bone.

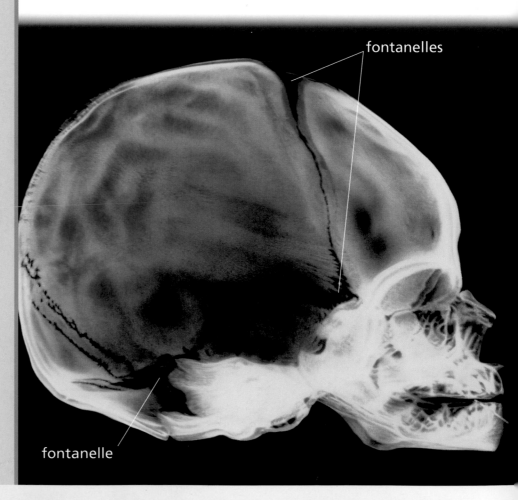

fontanelles

fontanelle

cartilage   tough, springy substance. It covers the ends of bones inside a joint. It also forms some parts of the skeleton.

Changing and mending

Bones do not stay exactly the same shape. Repeating a movement often can make muscles and bones bigger. Right-handed people often have bigger bones in their right arms and hands.

Bones can mend themselves if they break. But mending happens more quickly when we are young. This is because the bones are still growing.

Put back together

Doctors need to put a broken bone back together as perfectly as possible. Otherwise the bone will heal in the wrong shape.

◄ Some bones in a baby's skull are not yet joined together. There are gaps between them. These gaps are called fontanelles.

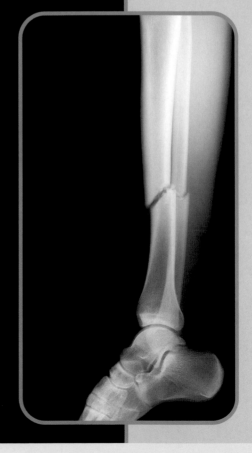

Flexi-body

Your skeleton is strong and tough. But you wouldn't be able to move an inch without joints.

A joint is where two or more bones meet. Your body has more than 200 joints. Most of them let you bend or straighten parts of your body. This happens when your muscles pull on the bones.

New joints for old

Some people, suffer from stiff, painful joints. Doctors can remove the worn parts. They replace them with joints made of metal and plastic (see below).

This baseball player ➤ pitches the ball. She uses her elbow, wrist, and finger joints to do this.

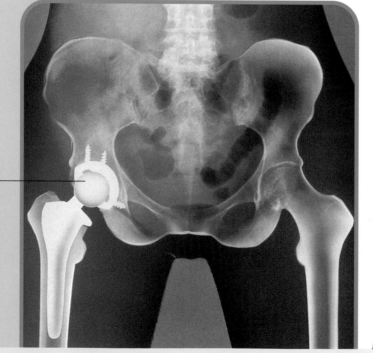

plastic hip joint

Body language   sprain   when a joint is forced to move too far, damaging the soft parts

Bendy – but not that bendy

Most of the body's joints can only move a certain amount. Sometimes the bones are forced too far. This causes damage, swelling, and pain. It is called a sprained joint. For example, you can **sprain** a joint when you "twist" your ankle.

Joints with no point?

You have joints in your body that can't move. These are called **sutures**. You have some in your **skull**. Wiggly lines (see below) mark where bones are fixed together.

sutures

sutures   fixed joints, where bones have joined solidly together

21

Smooth moves

The body's joints usually work smoothly and quietly. This is because of the way they are made.

First, the ends of joint bones have a covering of **cartilage**. Cartilage is smooth, shiny, and slippery. Bare bones would rub each other when the joint moved. Cartilage allows the bones to slip past each other.

Inside a joint

A body joint and its fluid are contained in a kind of bag. This is called the **joint capsule** (see below).

The knee has extra cartilage between the bones. This gives extra protection. ▼

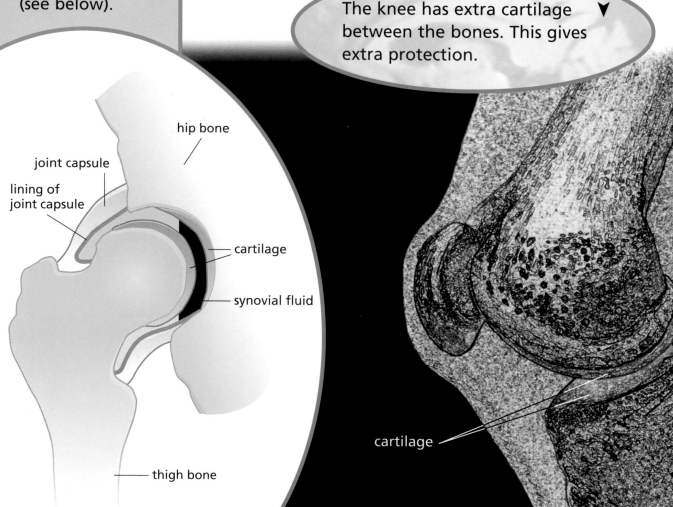

hip bone

joint capsule

lining of joint capsule

cartilage

synovial fluid

thigh bone

cartilage

Body language   joint capsule   bag-like part around the bone ends in a joint. It contains a slippery fluid.

Oil in the body machine

Second, body joints have "oil" inside. This makes the parts in the joint move easily. The oil is called **synovial fluid**.

Third, joints have **ligaments**. These are like strong elastic bands around the joint. They stop the bones moving too far apart.

Joint designs

The body has different types of joints. The joints are for different movements. Each type of joint has a name.

	Type of joint	Movement	Examples
	Hinge	Back and forward	Knee, elbow, smaller knuckles
	Ball-and-socket	Lots of movement including twisting	Shoulder, hip
	Saddle	Back and forward, side-to-side	Base of the thumb
	Gliding	Some sliding	Small bones of wrist, ankle
	Pivot	Turning or spinning so head can turn	Top of backbone under **skull**

synovial fluid slippery fluid that works like oil in a joint

Get a move on!

Joints need to be used. Your joints get stiff if you don't exercise. They stop moving smoothly. They might even ache or cause pain. Regular exercise can stop this getting worse.

On guard!

People doing fast–moving sports should wear protective guards over joints. These help protect the skin and joints.

Sports players are ➤ careful to rest any injured joints. Playing on with joint damage can cause trouble in the future.

Body language   osteoarthritis   painful, stiff joints. It is usually caused by
worn-out cartilage.

How much is too much?

But joints can be used too much. People such as athletes and sports players take special care. They try not to over-use their joints. Otherwise lots of small injuries can happen. Then **cartilage** in the joint gets rough and flaky. This is known as **osteoarthritis**. It causes pain and stiffness.

When a joint "pops out"

Sometimes the bones in a joint slip apart. This is called a **dislocation** (shown below). It is very painful. But a doctor can move the bones back into place.

JOINT FACTS

Biggest joint: the knee

Smallest joint: the one on the tiny stirrup bone deep inside the ear. It is smaller than this "o".

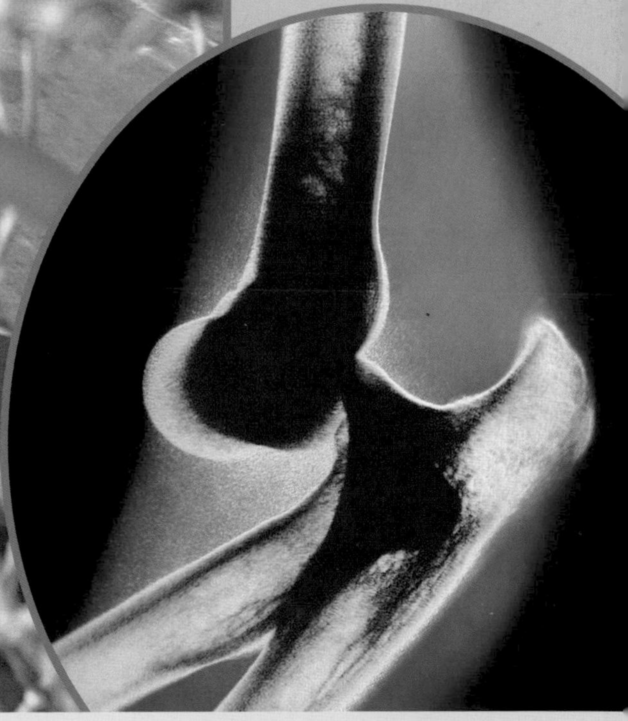

dislocation when bones in a joint move too far and come out of position

Muscling in

Layers of muscles

The left side of this picture shows muscles just under the skin. Beneath them is another set of muscles. The right side of the picture shows some of these. Under them is a third layer of muscles. They are right next to the skeleton.

Bones hold you up, but muscles make you move. Muscles have one simple task. This is to get shorter, or **contract**.

You have about 640 muscles in your body. Most are attached to bones at each end. When the muscle gets shorter, it pulls the bones closer together. This causes movement.

contract   become smaller or shorter. When a muscle contracts it pulls on the bones attached to it.

Biggest, smallest

Muscles come in different shapes and sizes. The biggest are the gluteus maximus muscles. These are powerful muscles in your bottom. They pull the thigh bones backwards when you walk, run, or jump.

The smallest muscle is deep inside your ear. This is the stapedius muscle. It is as thin as cotton thread. It pulls on the tiniest bone in your body.

◄ Muscles move the body. They can also keep it in position. This diver's muscles hold his body in position as he falls through the air.

Team work

Muscles work as groups. You use about 40 muscles just to turn over this page! These are in your hand and fingers. You also use arm and shoulder muscles. These help put your hand in the right place.

Most muscles become narrower at each end. This rope-like part is called a **tendon**.

Inside a muscle

Each muscle is made up of lots of rod-like fibres. These are myofibres (see below). They are about as thick as hairs.

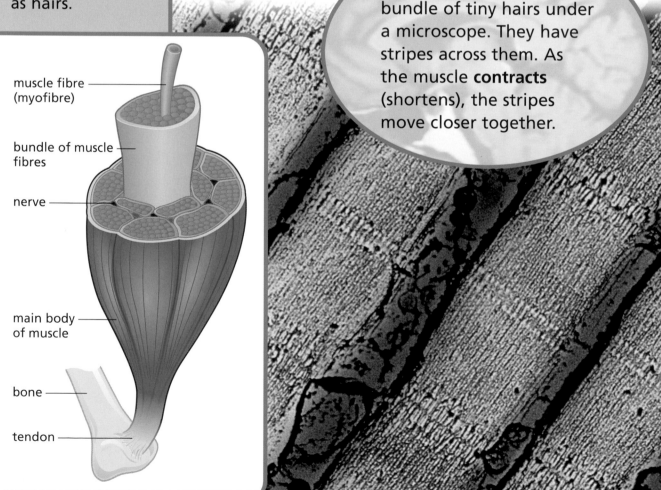

muscle fibre (myofibre)

bundle of muscle fibres

nerve

main body of muscle

bone

tendon

A muscle looks like a ▼ bundle of tiny hairs under a microscope. They have stripes across them. As the muscle **contracts** (shortens), the stripes move closer together.

tendon   narrow end part of a muscle that joins to a bone

The tendon is fixed firmly to the bone. When the muscles shorten, the tendon pulls the bone.

No push, only pull

But muscles can only pull. They can't push. When you move, one set of muscles gets smaller. They pull on the bone. The sets of muscles that aren't pulling the bone relax and stretch out.

Bigger muscles

We all have about 640 muscles. Bodybuilders and weightlifters have the same number of muscles. But their muscles are bigger than normal. They have more of the tiny fibres inside.

Turn that frown upside-down!

Your face and head contain more than 60 muscles. These muscles can change the expression on your face. They can make you look angry, happy, and sad. They can show many other feelings too.

Smile away

It really is easier to smile than to frown. Smiling uses about 18 face muscles. Frowning uses over 40. Making each muscle shorter uses energy. So save energy by smiling!

Muscle-to-muscle

Some face muscles are not joined to bones. They are joined to other muscles instead. As one **contracts** (shortens), it changes the shape of the other muscles.

Seven muscles meet at the corner of your mouth. When one moves, it affects the others. This is how your mouth can make so many shapes.

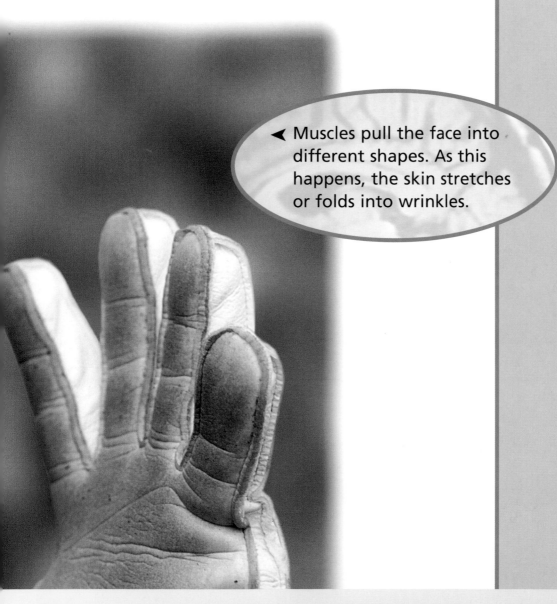

◄ Muscles pull the face into different shapes. As this happens, the skin stretches or folds into wrinkles.

contract   become smaller or shorter. When a muscle contracts it pulls the bones attached to it.

Munching muscles

Eating uses two main face muscles. One runs from above the ear to the lower jaw. The other runs from the cheekbone to the lower jaw. Both muscles pull up the lower jaw as you bite and chew.

Bendiest muscle

Your tongue is almost all muscle. Some people can curl it into a "U"!

One of your main eating muscles is in your lips. It has two parts. There is one part in each lip. Your lips close when the muscle shortens.

It's all talk

You use about 40 muscles when you speak. These are in your chest, neck, **voicebox**, throat, and mouth.

Chest muscles push air up from your lungs. The air goes through your voicebox. This is where sounds are made.

Voicebox muscles work to make the sounds high or low. Face, tongue, and lip muscles change the shape of your mouth. This allows you to say words clearly.

Blink, wink

Your two busiest face muscles control your eyelids. They work about 30,000 times a day. When both these muscles shorten, your eyes blink. When only one shortens, you wink.

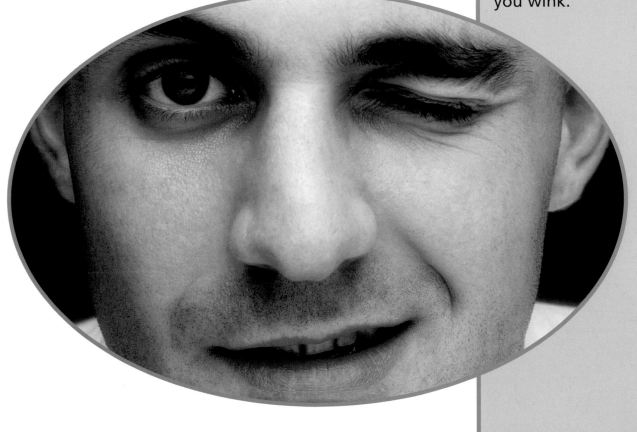

voicebox   part where the sounds of the voice are made

Go for it – every day

Muscles, bones, and joints are meant to be used. Muscles that aren't used regularly become floppy. They also become weak. Then they are not able to pull hard.

Muscles make your heart beat. They also make your lungs breathe. These muscles benefit from exercise too.

When you're active

When you're very active, more blood flows to your muscles. Your heart has to pump hard to supply this blood. You also breathe a lot more air each minute. This extra work helps keep your heart, lungs, and muscles healthy.

Day by day

You don't need special equipment to exercise. You can exercise by walking or cycling. Some of the best exercises are swimming and dancing.

Using muscles is not ➤ just healthy. Exercise and sport make many people feel happier.

Warm up, cool down

Athletes always do warm-up exercises before an event. These get the muscles warm and flexible. Otherwise sudden movements may cause injury.

Let's work together

Bones support and protect the body. Muscles move bones. Joints let the bones move easily. These three **body systems** work together as we walk and talk.

They work together as we carry out hundreds of other actions too. For example, imagine you're walking past people playing ball. Suddenly the ball is coming towards your head.

Jumping high

High-jumping uses the largest muscle in the body. This is the gluteus maximus. It is in your bottom. It pulls the thigh back to push the body upwards.

body system   various parts that work together to carry out one main task

Look out!

Straight away you close your eyes and screw up your face. You protect your face with your hands. You lean away from the ball.

All this happens in a second. Muscles, bones, and joints work together to make these actions. They work to protect you.

▼ A simple ball-throwing action uses more than 30 bones. It also uses 50 joints, and 100 muscles. These are in the shoulder, arm, hand, and fingers.

All under control

You use bones, muscles, and joints to make a movement. You also use your brain. The brain controls muscles. It tells them when to **contract**, or shorten. It also tells them how much to contract.

The brain does this by sending signals to muscles. It sends signals along wire-like parts. These parts are called **nerves**.

Nerve signals

Motor end plates (see below) spread nerve signals through the muscle. This makes the muscle fibres contract.

Sometimes we have to carry out delicate ➤ movements. We watch them carefully. We correct a movement that isn't quite right. We do this by adjusting the muscle.

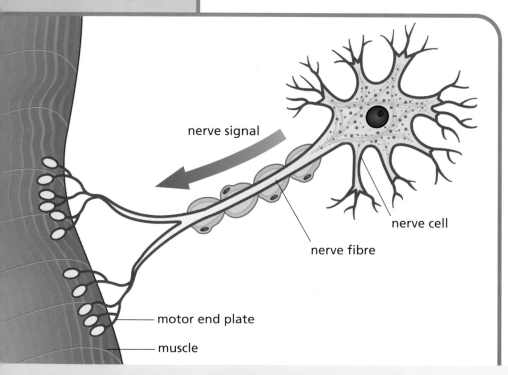

nerve signal

nerve cell

nerve fibre

motor end plate

muscle

motor end plate place where nerve fibres join muscles

In the brain

A movement starts as a signal inside the brain. It begins in the **motor centre** (see diagram below). The signal goes to another part of the brain. This is the **cerebellum**.

The cerebellum sends hundreds of signals to different muscles. It makes sure the muscles all work together smoothly.

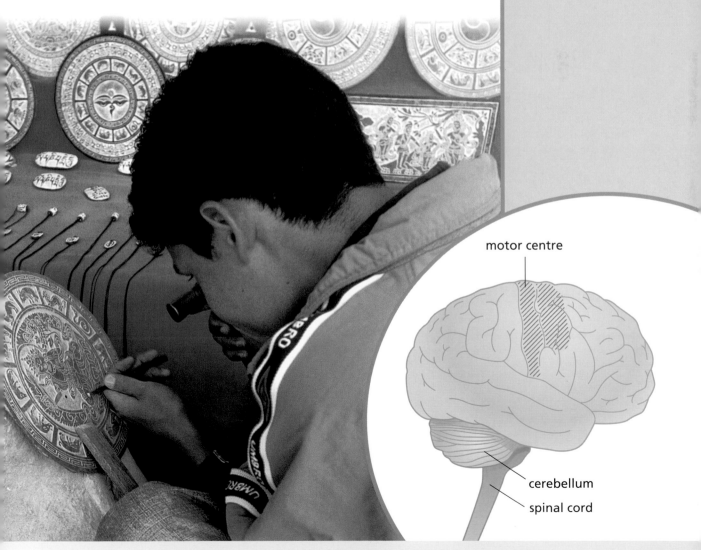

motor centre

cerebellum

spinal cord

cerebellum   part at the back of the brain that makes sure muscles work together smoothly

Auto muscles

What involuntary muscles do

- ✦ **Gullet** – squeeze food into the stomach
- ✦ **Stomach** – mash food up
- ✦ **Guts** – push food along
- ✦ **End of guts** – hold solid waste until you use the toilet
- ✦ **Bladder** – hold urine (liquid waste) until you use the toilet

There are three types of muscle in your body. All the ones mentioned so far are called skeletal muscles. This is because most are joined to bones of the skeleton. They are also known as **voluntary muscles**. This is because you volunteer, or decide, to move them.

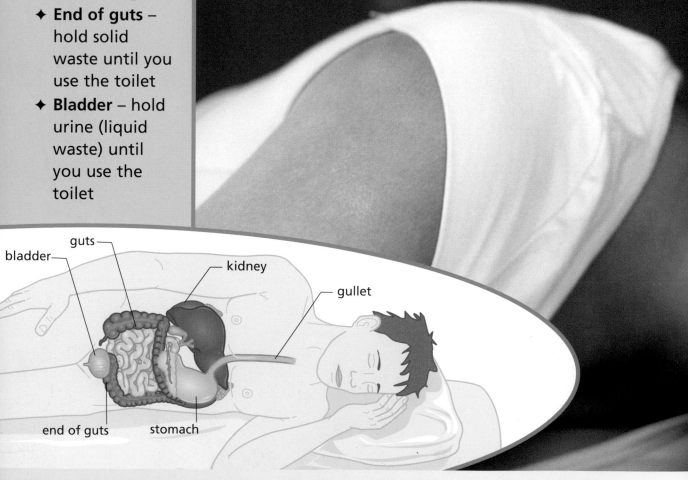

bladder

guts

kidney

gullet

end of guts

stomach

voluntary muscles muscles that work when we want them to. They do not work automatically.

Muscles inside

There is a second kind of muscle called smooth muscle. It is also known as **involuntary muscle**. This is because you don't have to think about moving it.

Involuntary muscle is found in parts such as your stomach and guts. It is in the walls of these parts. It squashes food in the stomach. It squeezes food through the guts.

▼ Most skeletal muscles relax when you sleep. But muscles are busy inside your body. Some of them are helping to break down food.

A very special muscle

The third type of muscle keeps your whole body alive. It is **cardiac** muscle. Cardiac muscle makes up the walls of your heart.

The heart muscle **contracts** (gets smaller) to squeeze blood out. It squeezes blood out into tubes called arteries. **Arteries** take the blood around the body.

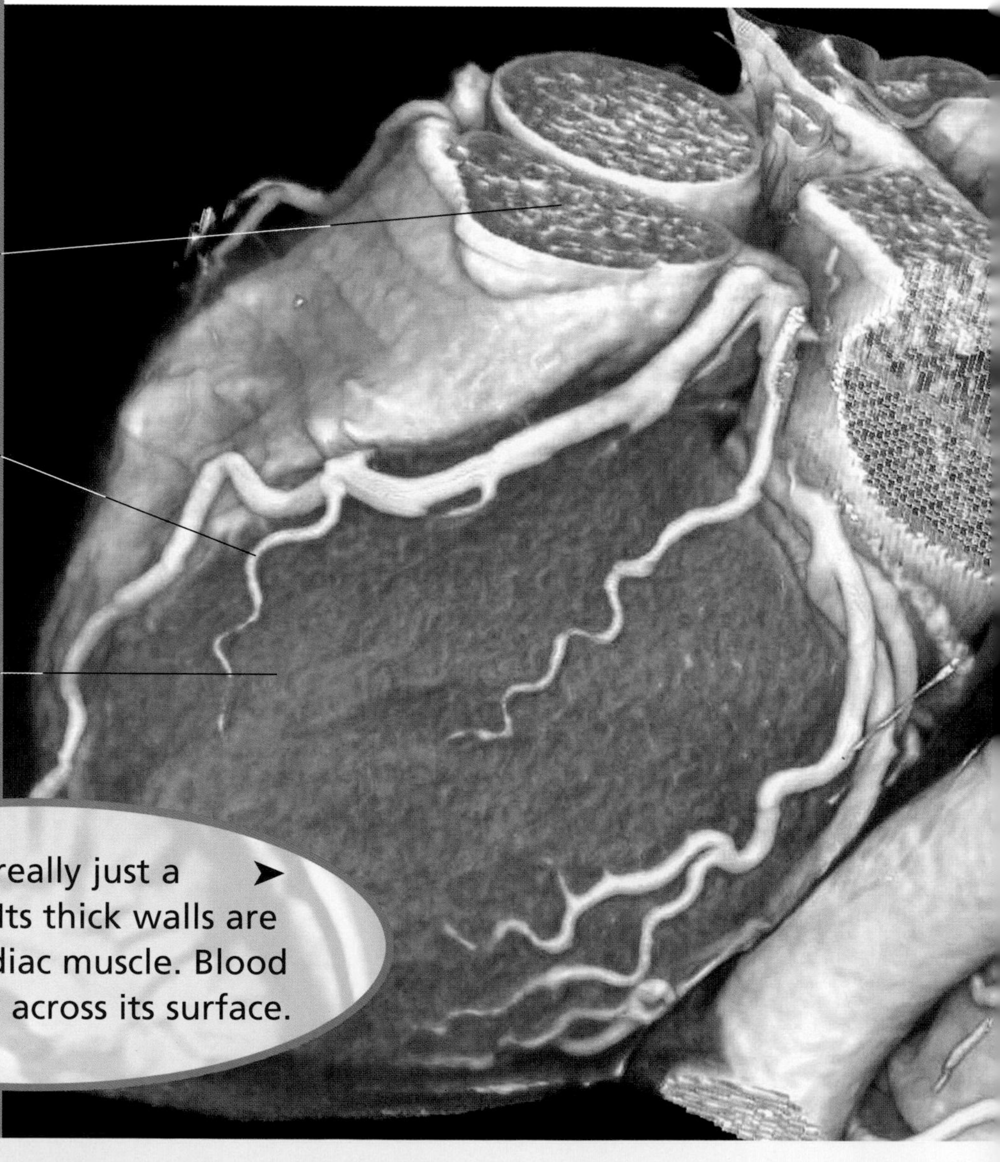

large blood vessel

small blood vessel

heart walls made of cardiac muscle

The heart is really just a hollow bag. Its thick walls are made of cardiac muscle. Blood vessels snake across its surface. ➤

When the heart muscle relaxes, blood flows into the heart. It flows in through tubes called **veins**.

Never tired

The heart muscle never stops working. Unlike other muscles, it doesn't get tired. But like other muscles, it needs blood to make it work. Small blood vessels carry blood to the heart muscles.

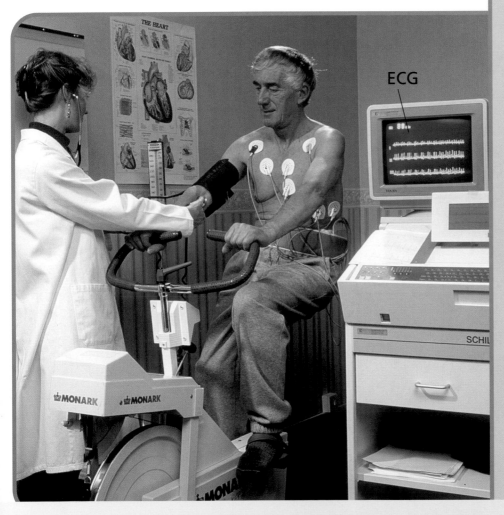

ECG

Spiky lines

Working muscles give out electricity (a form of **energy**). An ECG (electro-cardiogram) machine picks up electricity from heart muscles. The machine shows this as wavy or spiky lines (see left). Unusual patterns may be a sign of heart trouble.

arteries   large blood vessels that carry blood away from the heart

Find out more

Did you know?

Bone is amazingly strong. But it is also light. If your skeleton was made of steel, it would weigh five times more. A skeleton of wood, plastic, or aluminium might be as light as bone. But it would not be as strong.

Books

Muscles: Injury, Illness and Health, Carol Ballard (Heinemann Library, 2003)

Are You Tough Enough?, Paul Mason (Raintree, 2005)

Training for the Top: Nutrition and Exercise, Paul Mason (Raintree, 2005)

Understanding Your Muscles and Bones: Internet Linked, Rebecca Treays (Usborne, 2006)

World Wide Web

The Internet can tell you more about your body and your brain. You can use a search engine or search directory.

Type in keywords such as:

- bones
- diet and fitness
- muscles
- nervous system
- human brain

Search tips

There are billions of pages on the Internet. It can be difficult to find what you are looking for.

These search skills will help you find useful websites more quickly:

- Know exactly what you want to find out about.
- Use two to six keywords in a search. Put the most important words first.
- Only use names of people, places or things.

Where to search

Search engine

A search engine looks through millions of pages. It lists all the sites that match the words in the search box. You will find the best matches are at the top of the list, on the first page. Try **bbc.co.uk/search**

Search directory

A person instead of a computer has sorted a search directory. You can search by keyword or subject and browse through the different sites. It is like looking through books on a library shelf. Try **yahooligans.com**

Glossary

arteries large blood vessels that carry blood away from the heart

blood vessels tubes that carry blood through the body

body system various parts that work together to carry out one main task

bone marrow jelly-like substance inside certain bones. It makes new blood cells and stores nutrients.

cardiac to do with the heart

cartilage tough, springy substance. It covers the ends of bones inside a joint. It also forms some parts of the skeleton.

cells microscopic "building blocks" that make up all body parts

cerebellum part at the back of the brain that makes sure muscles work together smoothly

collagen tough, string-like fibres found in body parts such as skin and bones

contract become smaller or shorter. When a muscle contracts it pulls the bones attached to it.

cranium domed upper part of the skull

dislocation when bones in a joint move too far and come out of position

energy ability to do work and make things happen

involuntary muscles muscles that work automatically, without us having to think about them

joint capsule bag-like part around bone ends in a joint. It contains a slippery fluid.

ligament "strap" that holds bones together at a joint and stops them moving too far

minerals substances, such as iron and calcium, that the body needs to stay healthy

motor centre region at the top of the brain, that controls muscle movement

motor end plate place where nerve fibres join muscle fibres

nerves string-like parts that carry messages around the body

osteoarthritis painful, stiff joints. It is usually caused by worn-out cartilage.

oxygen gas that makes up one-fifth of air

red blood cells cells that carry oxygen around the body

skull main bone inside the head. It is really more than 20 separate bones joined firmly together.

spinal cord main nerve linking the brain to the rest of the body

spine body's central support column. It is also called the backbone.

sprain when a joint is forced to move too far, damaging the soft parts

sutures fixed joints, where bones have joined solidly together

synovial fluid slippery fluid that works like oil in a joint

tendon narrow end part of a muscle that joins to a bone

vein large blood vessel that carries blood to the heart

vertebrae individual bones of the backbone, which join like links in a chain

voicebox part where the sounds of the voice are made

voluntary muscles muscles that work when we want them to. They do not work automatically.

white blood cells pale cells in the blood that clean blood and fight germs and diseases

Index

Titles in the *Freestyle Express: Body Talk* series include:

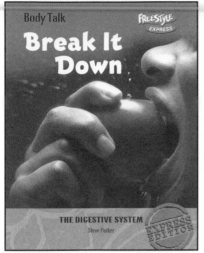

Hardback   1-406-20414-5

Hardback   1-406-20415-3

Hardback   1-406-20419-6

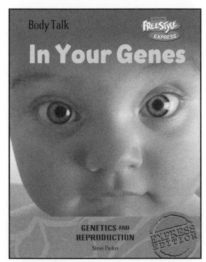

Hardback   1-406-20416-1

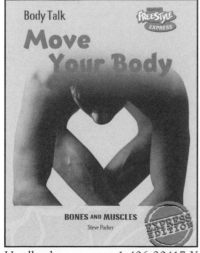

Hardback   1-406-20417-X

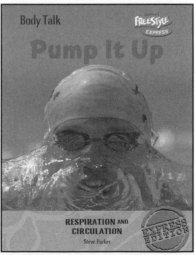

Hardback   1-406-20418-8

Find out about the other titles in this series on our website www.raintreepublishers.co.uk